A *season* of *sundays*

Images of the 2015 Gaelic Games year by the Sportsfile team of
photographers, with text by Alan Milton

An official GAA publication, published by Sportsfile

MATCH DAY TEAM MATES

SUPPORTING THE GAA FOR 25 YEARS

Carroll's reach the quarter-century milestone

Carroll's is proud to sponsor *A Season of Sundays* again this year. This has been a memorable year for Carroll's, marking the quarter-century milestone of the company's support for Gaelic games in our home county of Offaly.

For 25 years now – since 1991, the beginning of county jersey sponsorship in the GAA – Carroll's has been the only name emblazoned across the Offaly hurling and football teams' jerseys.

While Kilkenny and Dublin recorded thrilling and memorable All-Ireland senior hurling and football victories in 2015, the season was filled with soaring highs and inevitable lows for counties, clubs and schools nationwide.

Carroll's continues to show its commitment to Gaelic games by supporting clubs and schools of all sizes across the country. To acknowledge this long association with football and hurling, in 2015 we presented 25 full sets of jerseys to clubs and schools nationwide.

This practical initiative has enabled club and schools teams, small and large, to wear their own colours and encourages them to be proud of the communities they represent.

Carroll's is an Irish company with a proud heritage. Using our traditional recipes, we in Carroll's take our time to get it right. A Carroll's ham is carefully nurtured, hand-crafted and uses only the highest quality pork, which is slow cooked for a better taste.

Proud of our roots, Carroll's is fully committed to giving something back to the community, and our continued support of Gaelic games and *A Season of Sundays* is proof of that commitment.

We hope you enjoyed a Carroll's ham sandwich on your way to and from matches, big and small, this year and we are certain that 2016 will also be a season of success.

The Carroll's Team

sportsfile PUBLISHING

Published by:
SPORTSFILE
Patterson House, 14 South Circular Road
Portobello, Dublin 8, Ireland
www.sportsfile.com

Photographs:
Copyright © 2015 Sportsfile

ISBN: 978-1-905468-29-4

Text:
Alan Milton

Editing:
Eddie Longworth

Quotations research:
Seán Creedon

Additional photographs:
Barry Cregg, Eóin Noonan, Mark Marlow, Ray Ryan

Design:
The Design Gang, Tralee

Colour reproduction:
Mark McGrath

Print production:
PB Print Solutions

Case Binding:
Robinson & Mornin Bookbinders Ltd, Belfast

The Sportsfile photographic team:

Brendan Moran
Cody Glenn
Dáire Brennan
David Maher
Diarmuid Greene
Matt Browne
Oliver McVeigh
Pat Murphy
Paul Mohan
Piaras Ó Mídheach
Ramsey Cardy
Ray McManus
Sam Barnes
Seb Daly
Stephen McCarthy
Tomás Greally

There will be days like this...

Days like this. It's fascinating to observe the contrasting celebrations of victorious teams in the dressingroom at Croke Park on All-Ireland final day. The privileged few who gain entrance see players dancing, singing, shouting and generally larking about – mayhem breaks out.

The atmosphere is always joyous and wild, but this year I noticed that some celebrations are wilder than others.

Last September in the Kilkenny dressingroom, there was a brilliant sense of victory and companionship as they joined in a circle around the Liam MacCarthy Cup and had a sing-song. Not surprisingly, *The Rose of Mooncoin* led the charge.

Rackard Cody, the Kilkenny bagman, went around decorating the players with the gold ribbons he had saved from the pitch. I doubt if he actually collected them – more likely he removed them from the boots of the players who had celebrated on the pitch a little earlier.

Just two weeks later, drowned like a scalded cat after spending hours in the rain, I was in the same warm-up area of the same dressingroom that had welcomed the Kilkenny hurlers and in bounced the victorious Dublin footballers with the Sam Maguire Cup.

Michael Darragh Macauley headed straight to a massive loudspeaker and connected an iPhone

All hell broke loose as Van Morrison's *Days Like This* blasted out. It prompted a massive dance session and most joined in the sing-song. The players went ballistic when the choir boys came to the line *'Well my mama told me there'll be days like this'*.

The atmosphere was electric – if there was an All-Ireland championship for the best dressingroom celebration, Dublin would be the undisputed kings. Players live for days like this.

Not alone are there days like these but there are books like this because there are generous sponsors like Carroll's. They are long-time sponsors of the GAA in Offaly and, once again, I'd like to thank them for their support of *A Season of Sundays*.

Ray McManus

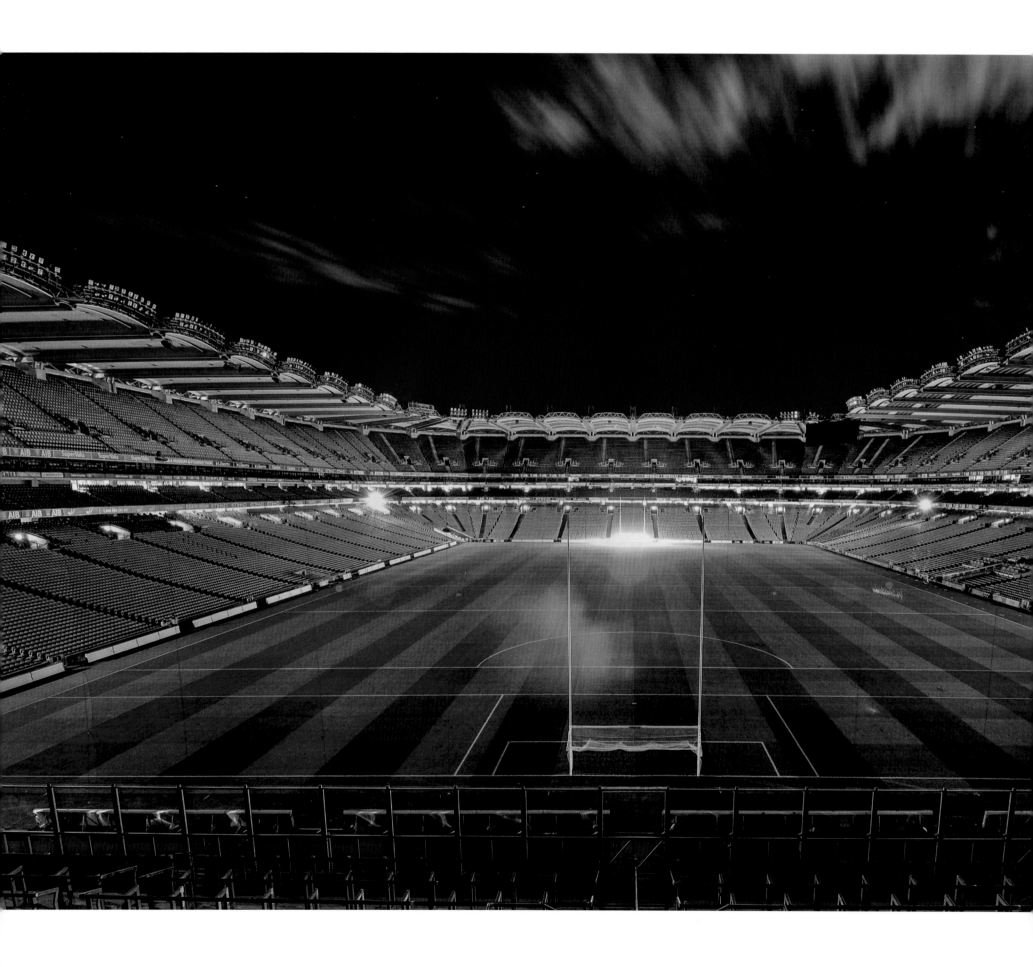

The defining images of a memorable season

Is cúis mhór áthais dom an réamhrá a scríobh don fhoilseachán iontach seo i mo chéad bhliain mar Uachtarán Chumann Lúthchleas Gael.

Ní dóigh liom go bhfuil aon leabhar eile a thugann léiriú níos soléire ar an aoibhneas agus ar an taibhseacht a bhaineann le séasúr iomaíochta CLG ná a thugann an leabhar seo, ní amháin i mbliana ach chuile bhliain.

The last vestiges of 2015 are upon us, the great games and heroics of another wonderful year are fading embers and those teams lucky enough to receive honours and accolades for their efforts can bask in the afterglow that only the sense of achievement provides.

Of course they are in the minority – and therein lies the rub. Hope springs eternal on an annual basis, not just in our codes but in sport in general.

A line will be drawn under the activity of 2015 and the gaze will turn to a new campaign, fresh opportunities, new personalities and different faces.

Success is measured in different ways. Quite often a league or provincial breakthrough sates the appetite. For the big hitters, those traditionally associated with podium appearances, it generally requires something later in the summer to satisfy them.

On that front 2015 left us with two renowned heavyweights as the last teams standing.

Kilkenny emerged on top in hurling with a second-half display in the All-Ireland final that left us marvelling at their winning ways. In football, Dublin saw off old foes Kerry in a downpour to claim a third title in five years.

However, to reduce the season to these two highlights would be to sell it short.

At this time of year we all delve into the memory file for the moments that made us laugh, smile or grimace. Was it a club game, a schools outing to Croke Park or some other county ground? Was it a league promotion or title success, a provincial challenge that reached the intended destination or one that fell agonisingly short?

In keeping with every season, some of the same images jump out. All-Ireland club champions Corofin and Ballyhale Shamrocks claimed St Patrick's Day at Croke Park as their own with displays so assured that no one could question their entitlement to silverware.

Waterford's young hurlers demanded our attention during a captivating league campaign that culminated in victory over Cork in the final in Thurles. Although they didn't scale the championship summit, Munster final and All-Ireland semi-final appearances hint at their huge potential.

Westmeath provided many of us with the stand-out comeback and result of the year – all on the same day. Reactions reveal a lot in sport and the responses of both players and maroon-clad supporters to their Leinster semi-final success over Meath will live long in the memory. Meanwhile, Monaghan's excellence in Ulster continued as they captured another title.

The All-Ireland semi-finals excelled, with the Galway and Tipperary hurlers producing a game for the ages and the football clashes of Tyrone and Kerry and Dublin and Mayo living up to their pre-match billings.

The final word went to the ladies of Cork – not once but twice – as a dynasty of unquestionable substance yielded camogie and football honours for two special groups of players.

However, the memories of these games should not be the preserve of those who had the privilege of witnessing them first hand. To that end the constant presence of the Sportsfile photographic team on sidelines across the island – and indeed further afield – serves us well.

They catch the obvious images and of course the less obvious ones, the sublime and the incredible. Like the players, managers and supporters, they are present in all weathers, long before and long after games.

In each of the last 19 years, Ray McManus has provided the GAA with a valued account of the season's activities. It is a page-by-page chronicle in pictures – and some words – of campaigns that we live our lives by. The images are all striking – some in their simplicity, some in their beauty.

Season 2015: seen through the prism that is *A Season of Sundays*.

Le gach dea ghuí,

Aogán Ó Fearghail

AOGÁN Ó FEARGHAIL
UACHTARÁN CHUMANN LÚTHCHLEAS GAEL

1 Dublin Bus / The Herald Hurling Challenge - Parnells GAA Club, Dublin
Dublin 2-13   Dubs Stars 3-18

Dublin Bus / The Herald Football Challenge - Parnells GAA Club, Dublin
Dublin 2-21   Dubs Stars 1-11

2.

(1) New year, and the same starting platform that is the
Annual Dubs Stars matches. Dublin's new hurling manager
Ger Cunningham gets an early look at capital talent

(2) Gong secured, the Dublin footballers conduct their
warm-down against a grey January sky

3 Bank of Ireland Dr. McKenna Cup - St. Mary's Park, Castleblayney
Monaghan 0-20   UU Jordanstown 2-10

4 Bank of Ireland Dr. McKenna Cup - Athletic Grounds, Armagh
Armagh 1-10   Tyrone 1-12

Bank of Ireland Dr. McKenna Cup - Páirc Esler, Newry
Down 1-09   Cavan 2-11

Bord na Móna O'Byrne Cup - Blessington GAA Club, Co. Wicklow
Wicklow 2-14   IT Carlow 2-09

1.

2.

3.

4.

(1) Lights, Camera, Action. Monaghan pose for an early-season team photo ahead of their Dr McKenna Cup game against Jordanstown in the impressive surroundings of Castleblayney

(2) Instructions crisp and clear, just like the January weather. Kieran McGeeney – embarking on a new phase of his managerial career, a return home to Armagh – gives Finnian Moriarty his riding instructions

(3) Another newbie. Down manager Jim McCorry looks light on his feet ahead of his first assignment, a home reversal against Cavan at Páirc Esler

(4) Fáílte isteach. Intercounty management begins for former Dublin footballer Johnny Magee in his neighbouring Garden County. Michael Sargent, chairman of the Blessington club, marks the occasion before a home win over IT Carlow

4 FBD League - Enniscrone-Kilglass GAA Club, Co. Sligo
Sligo 0-05 Galway 0-14

Bank of Ireland Dr. McKenna Cup - Owenbeg Centre of Excellence, Dungiven
Derry 1-16 Donegal 0-08

1.

(1) Aim for the skies. Eddie Hoare bisects the posts in front of a stunning backdrop as Galway make the most of a visit to the Enniscrone-Kilglass club to beat Sligo

(2) Under the shadow of the Sperrins. Supporters are dwarfed by their surroundings at the Owenbeg Centre of Excellence in Dungiven as Derry set the pace against Donegal

2.

7 Bord na Móna O'Byrne Cup - Páirc Tailteann, Navan
Meath 1-17   Longford 1-09

Bord na Móna O'Byrne Cup - Parnell Park, Dublin
Dublin 0-17   Offaly 0-13

Bord na Móna O'Byrne Cup - Geraldine Park, Athy
Kildare 2-07   Carlow 1-09

1.

2.

3.

(1) Dim lights and heavy clothing. Meath limber up before a successful outing against Longford in Páirc Tailteann

(2) There will be busier days. Dublin heavy-hitters Stephen Cluxton, Jack McCaffrey and Denis Bastick watch their team's win over Offaly. The trio would be centre stage thereafter as a memorable season unfolded

(3) Warm cuppa. Referee Stephen Johnson chats over tea with his umpires Jerry Corrigan, Mike Englishby, Brian Carroll and Robert Murray at half-time in Geraldine Park in Athy as Kildare narrowly beat Carlow

9 Waterford Crystal Cup - Dr. Morris Park, Thurles
Tipperary 4-16 Mary Immaculate College 1-16

11 McGrath Cup - Clonmel Sportsfield, Clonmel
Tipperary 0-12 Cork 1-14

1.

2.

(1) Full house. The Tipperary hurlers crowd into an ornate dugout in Dr Morris Park in Thurles as manager Eamon O'Shea gives the half-time team talk. Tipp prevail against Mary I

(2) Targetmen? Referee Richard Moloney, left, and match officials Johnny Murphy, centre, and Shane Florish see the funny side as they make their way to the field in Clonmel for Tipperary's home defeat to Cork

1.

2.

3.

11   Bord na Móna O'Byrne Cup - Páirc Uí Suíocháin, Gorey
Wexford 2-15   Wicklow 2-11

Bank of Ireland Dr. McKenna Cup - St Tiernach's Park, Clones
Monaghan 0-11   Down 1-12

McGrath Cup - Austin Stack Park, Tralee
Kerry 0-16   IT Tralee 4-12

FBD League - Philly McGuinness Park, Mohill, Co. Leitrim
Leitrim 1-09   Galway 0-13

4.

(1) The greenhouse effect. New Wexford football manager David Power finds his bearings ahead of his team's win over Wicklow in Gorey

(2) Leading from the front. Monaghan captain Drew Wylie leads his team on to the Clones pitch for their McKenna Cup game against Down

(3) Top dog for the day. Kerry under-21 manager Darragh Ó Sé, deputising in the absence of senior boss Éamonn Fitzmaurice, advises Paul Kennelly as a depleted Kerry lose to IT Tralee. Most of the All-Ireland champions are abroad on a team holiday

(4) Bunting in place means showtime. Paddy McGowan of Leitrim and Galway's Donal O'Neill contest the throw-in at Mohill. The hunched scoreboard operator reminds us that it's mid-winter

11 Bord na Móna O'Byrne Cup - St. Conleth's Park, Newbridge
Kildare 0-21   UCD 1-05

14 Bank of Ireland Dr. McKenna Cup - Athletic Grounds, Armagh
Armagh 2-11   St. Mary's, Belfast 0-14

17 Waterford Crystal Cup - John Fitzgerald Park, Kilmallock
Limerick 2-15   Waterford 1-15

1.

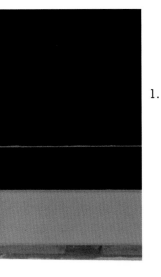
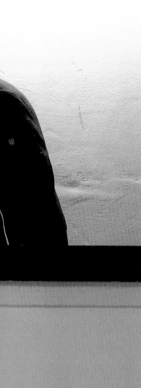

2.

3.

(1) Media centre. Kildare manager Jason Ryan does the post-match interviews following an O'Byrne Cup win over UCD in Newbridge while, next door, Pat Costello and Peter McConnon round up their radio analysis for Kfm

(2) Paradise for a night? Former Armagh manager and current selector Peter McDonnell, right, fills in for Kieran McGeeney for one night only. Assisted by Martin McQuillan, he steers the team to a home win over St Mary's

(3) As clear as mud. Waterford's Martin O'Neill, Austin Gleeson, Kevin Moran and Shane Bennett trudge off the Kilmallock pitch after their Waterford Crystal Cup reversal to Limerick

18 FBD League - Elverys MacHale Park, Castlebar
Mayo 1-10   Roscommon 2-12

McGrath Cup - Clashmore, Co. Waterford
Waterford 0-08   Cork 0-07

20 Walsh Cup - Parnell Park, Dublin
Dublin 4-20   DIT 1-12

21 Bank of Ireland Dr. McKenna Cup - Kingspan Breffni Park, Cavan
Cavan 1-08   Fermanagh 1-07

1.

2.

❝ It was a good tough game and we played some lovely football.
We had kept our powder dry for today **❞**

Roscommon manager John Evans after their first win over Mayo in Castlebar since 1986

4.

(1) Light and shadows. Roscommon players head to a well signposted warm-up area at MacHale Park in Castlebar before their FBD League win over Mayo

(2) Big clash in Clashmore. The gloves and hats - and the low scoring that follows - mean it's still January. Waterford edge Cork in McGrath Cup action

(3) 'You're new around here, yeah?' Parnell Park stalwart Patsy Kiernan converses with Corkman Ger Cunningham before Dublin's Walsh Cup win over DIT

(4) Schmoking. The Cavan players raise the ambient temperature in Breffni Park as they stand for Amhrán na bhFiann before pipping Fermanagh by a point

1.

2.

3.

" People have to be patient, the inside forwards have to be patient, the players on the ball have to be patient, and you have to use the width of the pitch rather than the centre "

Tyrone manager Mickey Harte on how they broke down Cavan's defensive system in the McKenna Cup final

24 Bank of Ireland Dr. McKenna Cup Final - Athletic Grounds, Armagh
Tyrone 1-13   Cavan 0-10

McGrath Cup Final - Fraher Field, Dungarvan
Waterford 3-12   UCC 1-09

25 Bord na Móna O'Byrne Cup Final - St Conleth's Park, Newbridge
Kildare 0-19   Dublin 0-24

FBD League Final - Kiltoom, Co. Roscommon
Roscommon 4-08   Galway 1-12

4.

(1) Different season, familiar sight. Tyrone captain Seán Cavanagh, with his four-year-old daughter Eva, celebrates the county's latest Dr McKenna Cup success, this time over Cavan

(2) Double act. Waterford twin brothers, captain Thomas O'Gorman, right, and Maurice, celebrate their McGrath Cup final success over UCC in Dungarvan

(3) Pre-match celebrations? Umpires Ryne Gough, left, and Dean Gough, cousins of match referee David, focus on the O'Byrne Cup before the Dublin v Kildare final in Newbridge

(4) Two legs good, six legs better. The Murtagh brothers, from left, Brian, Ciarán and Diarmuid, celebrate their FBD League final win over Galway in Kiltoom

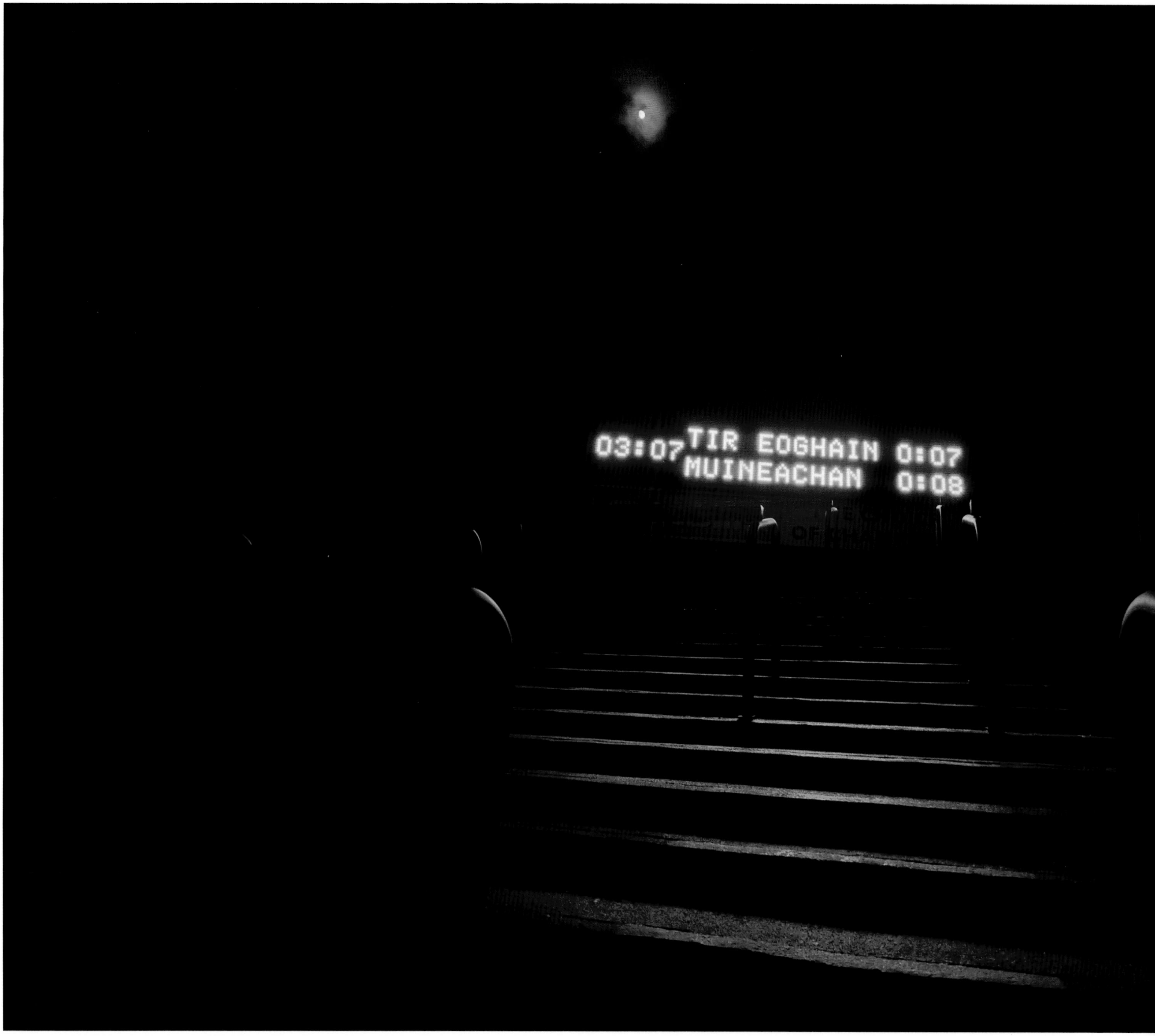
03:07
TIR EOGHAIN 0:07
MUINEACHAN 0:08

31 Allianz National Football League - Healy Park, Omagh
Tyrone 0-09   Monaghan 1-13

Allianz National Football League - MacCumhaill Park, Ballybofey
Donegal 1-15   Derry 0-12

Waterford Crystal Cup Final - Mallow GAA Grounds, Co. Cork
Limerick 3-20   Cork 1-16

1 Allianz National Football League - St. Conleth's Park, Newbridge
Kildare 1-15   Down 3-13

1.

2.

3.

4.

(1) Out of the darkness. The Healy Park floodlights fail for half an hour but the scoreboard continues to throw light on the situation, and confirm Monaghan's ascendancy against Tyrone in their league opener

(2) Bobble hats and beanie hats. Donegal manager Rory Gallagher addresses his troops who go on to defeat Derry at home in Gallagher's first league outing in charge

(3) Crystal by name and nature. Limerick captain Donal O'Grady receives the trophy after his team see off Cork in the Waterford Crystal Cup final in Mallow

(4) 'Tell me that one again.' Down's Conor Maginn shares a light moment with referee Anthony Nolan as the Ulstermen beat Kildare in Newbridge

1 Allianz National Football League - Athletic Grounds, Armagh
Armagh 2-08 Tipperary 0-13

Allianz National Football League - Kiltoom, Co. Roscommon
Roscommon 1-11 Cavan 0-14

7 Allianz National Football League - Páirc Tailteann, Navan
Meath 0-13 Kildare 0-11

Bord na Móna Walsh Cup Final - Croke Park, Dublin
Galway 1-22 Dublin 1-20

1.

2.

(1) Orchard in full bloom. Armagh's committed fans see their team get off on the right foot at the Athletic Grounds in their opening league date with Tipperary – though just about

(2) Holding on. Roscommon's Senan Kilbride clasps the ball as Micheál Lyng of Cavan tackles. A share of the spoils is the order of the day in Kiltoom

(3) Conserving energy. The Páirc Tailteann floodlights remain unlit – all the better to appreciate the magnificent skyline - but tickets are selling ahead of a Meath home win over neighbours Kildare

(4) The Walsh Cup at headquarters. Galway captain David Collins does the honours as his team see off Dublin in the first instalment of a Croke Park double-header

3.

4.

7   AIB GAA Hurling All-Ireland Senior Club Championship Semi-Final - O'Connor Park, Tullamore
Ballyhale Shamrocks 2-17   Gort 1-15

8   Allianz National Football League - Cusack Park, Mullingar
Westmeath 2-12   Galway 2-13

Allianz National Football League - County Grounds, Drogheda
Louth 1-16   Clare 0-13

1.

2.

(1) Sentry guards at gate 49. Ballyhale Shamrocks supporters
David Foley, aged six, and Brian Geraghty, five, follow their
team's progress against Gort from a slightly unorthodox
vantage point in Tullamore

(2) A clean sweep. Cusack Park steward Séamus McLoughlin,
from Moate, tidies the ground before the Westmeath-Galway
league game

(3) Studying the form. It's the County Grounds in Drogheda
– not the racecourse – as supporters check the programme
during the first half of Louth's win over Clare

8   Allianz National Football League - St. Mary's Park, Castleblayney
Monaghan 1-16   Cork 2-14

14   AIB GAA Football All-Ireland Senior Club Championship Semi-Final - O'Connor Park, Tullamore
Corofin 1-14   St. Vincent's 1-09

1.

2.

(1) Scouting mission completed, Monaghan defender Dessie Mone
returns to the dressingroom having inspected the pitch in Castleblayney.
Cork would go on to edge a lively encounter

(2) The eyes say it all. Shane Carthy tries to take in St Vincent's All-Ireland
club semi-final defeat to Corofin in Tullamore

1.

2.

3.

4.

" Mickey just had a quiet word with us at half-time, told us to keep calm and keep picking off the scores. That calming influence that Mickey has, that has been the big difference this year. "

Slaughtneil goalscorer Barry McGuigan is full of praise for manager Mickey Moran after their win over Austin Stacks in the All-Ireland club semi-final

15 Allianz National Hurling League - Parnell Park, Dublin
Dublin 2-20 Tipperary 0-14

AIB GAA Football All-Ireland Senior Club Championship Semi-Final - O'Moore Park, Portlaoise
Slaughtneil 1-14 Austin Stacks 2-10

21 Allianz National Hurling League - Fraher Field, Dungarvan
Waterford 3-21 Laois 0-12

22 Allianz National Hurling League - O'Connor Park, Tullamore
Offaly 0-12 Wexford 2-15

Allianz National Hurling League - Nowlan Park, Kilkenny
Kilkenny 3-11 Dublin 0-25

28 Allianz National Football League - Healy Park, Omagh
Tyrone 0-11 Derry 1-08

5.

6.

(1) Safety in numbers. Young Dubs search for a wayward sliotar at half-time in the county's opening-round league win over Tipperary at Parnell Park

(2) 'Croke Park on St Patrick's Day here we come.' Paudie McGuigan of Slaughtneil celebrates his team's All-Ireland club semi-final win over Austin Stacks in Portlaoise

(3) The B team? Joe Fitzpatrick leads his Laois team-mates from the B dressingroom at Dungarvan for the second half of a game that would run away from them

(4) Full-blooded aerial contest. Joe Bergin and Shane Kinsella of Offaly contest possession with Wexford's Jack Guiney and Paudie Foley. The visitors come out on top at O'Connor Park

(5) Something to ponder. Jackie Tyrrell, sans helmet, digests a home defeat to Dublin at Nowlan Park

(6) Ooooh or should that be arrrrrgh? Derry manager Brian McIver reacts to the play in the final minutes of a rain-soaked draw between his team and traditional rivals Tyrone at Healy Park

1 Allianz National Football League - Fitzgerald Stadium, Killarney
Kerry 0-15 Dublin 1-10

Allianz National Football League - St. Conleth's Park, Newbridge
Kildare 0-12 Westmeath 0-15

1.

2.

(1) Towering presence. Kerry's Kieran Donaghy and Denis Bastick of Dublin toss the coin with referee Eddie Kinsella and the full complement of umpires. Kerry shade a tetchy affair in Killarney, and the fixture would be revisited later in the year

(2) The home of the Lilywhites is … lilywhite. Referee Pádraig O'Sullivan makes tracks at a snow-covered St Conleth's Park before giving the meeting of Kildare and Westmeath the green light. The men in maroon claim the points

7 Allianz National Hurling League - O'Connor Park, Tullamore
Offaly 1-14   Waterford 2-18

Allianz National Football League - Croke Park, Dublin
Dublin 1-09   Tyrone 0-12

8 Allianz National Hurling League - Pearse Stadium, Salthill
Galway 0-20   Kilkenny 0-18

Allianz National Football League - Páirc Uí Rinn, Cork
Cork 3-17   Kerry 2-09

3.

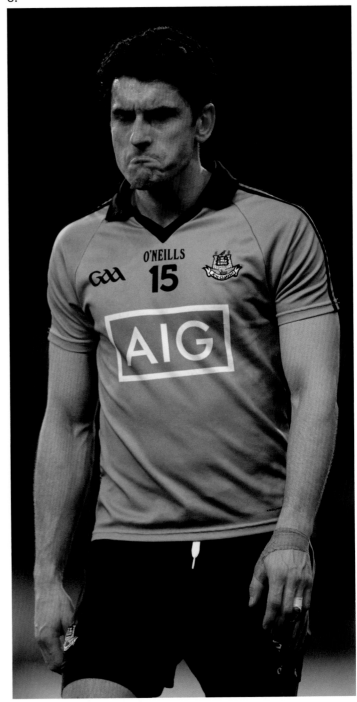

1.

2.

1) Arms race. Offaly defender David King grabs Shane Bennett in an attempt to steer the Waterford man away from goal. After a bright start, Offaly lose their way in Tullamore

(2) Outstretched arm, shortened grip. Joseph Cooney of Galway stretches every sinew in his effort to block Kilkenny's Cillian Buckley as Galway win in Salthill

(3) The expression says it all. Bernard Brogan grimaces as he leaves the pitch after a testing night against Tyrone in Croke Park when Dublin needed a late Dean Rock goal to salvage a draw

(4) Airborne for a calcium test. Johnny Buckley's bones stand up to the strain of Eoin Cadogan's attempted clearance. Kerry endure a chastening day by the Lee against a rampant Cork

1.

2.

3.

4.

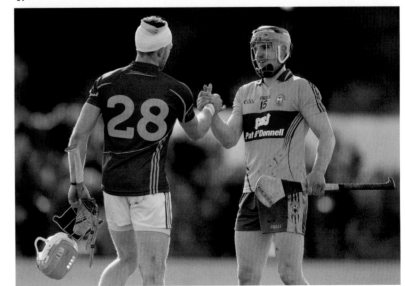

8 Allianz National Football League - O'Donnell Park, Letterkenny
Donegal 1-04   Monaghan 0-09

Allianz National Football League - Celtic Park, Derry
Derry 1-13   Mayo 2-12

Allianz National Hurling League - Wexford Park, Wexford
Wexford 3-18   Limerick 4-16

Allianz National Hurling League - Cusack Park, Ennis
Clare 0-20   Tipperary 2-19

14 Allianz National Football League - Elverys MacHale Park, Castlebar
Mayo 0-10   Dublin 2-18

Allianz National Football League - Páirc Tailteann, Navan
Meath 0-13   Laois 0-13

5.

6.

(1) Around the corner. Donegal's Karl Lacey kicks beyond the attempted block of Darren Hughes of Monaghan during an ultra-defensive game in Letterkenny that generated plenty of debate

(2) Held up in the tackle. Kevin McLoughlin keeps possession despite being enveloped by Derry's Benny Heron, left, and Kevin Johnston as Mayo collect two league points by the Foyle

(3) That's the job. Richie McCarthy and Stephen Walsh celebrate Limerick's away win over Wexford

(4) In the wars. Tipperary's Pádraic Maher shakes hands with Clare's John Conlon after Tipp's win in Ennis

(5) Shadow boxing? Dublin manager Jim Gavin is welcomed to MacHale Park in Castlebar by steward Richard O'Hallaron. Dublin cut loose on the night against Mayo but the two counties would captivate the nation before year's end

(6) One for the digital library. Parents take pictures of their young footballers after the half-time exhibition game in Navan. The main event, between Meath and Laois, ends in a dramatic draw

15 Allianz National Hurling League - St Tiernach's Park, Clones
Monaghan 0-18 Fingal 2-12

Allianz National Hurling League - Healy Park, Omagh
Tyrone 1-20 Louth 2-07

Allianz National Hurling League - Cusack Park, Mullingar
Westmeath 1-22 Wicklow 2-10

Allianz National Football League - County Grounds, Drogheda
Louth 3-11 Tipperary 4-16

3.

1.

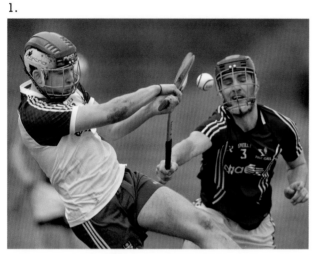

2.

(1) Flexible ash. Hurleys bend in Clones as Fingal's Graham Morris tries to block Fergal Rafter of Monaghan in the counties' draw

(2) In flight. Darren Hanrahan of Louth controls the sliotar with Conor Grogan and Tiernan Morgan in pursuit. Tyrone see off the visitors' challenge in Omagh

(3) Fully equipped. Seaghan Óg Collins of Mullingar, son of Westmeath hurling goalkeeper Peter Collins, steals the show at half-time during the home team's win over Wicklow

(4) Nowhere to run. Louth's Bevan Duffy challenges the odds in Drogheda where, from left, Tipperary's Barry Grogan, Séamus Kennedy, Ger Mulhare and Peter Acheson eye up his red jersey – and the ball

4.

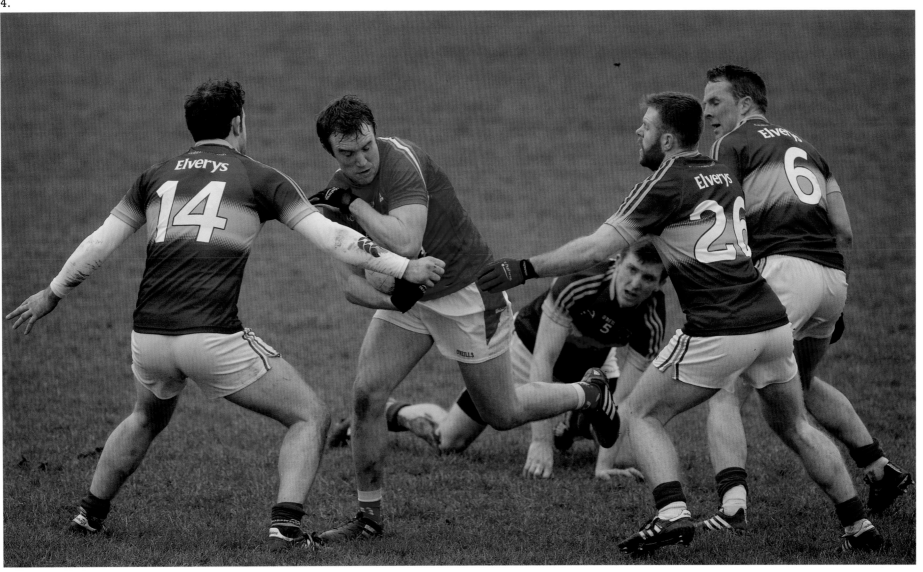

15 Allianz National Football League - Pearse Stadium, Salthill
Galway 0-10   Cavan 0-12

Allianz National Hurling League - Semple Stadium, Thurles
Tipperary 2-22   Kilkenny 1-13

Allianz National Football League - Austin Stack Park, Tralee
Kerry 2-13   Donegal 2-11

1.

2.

(1) Selfie 1. The days are long gone when a photo op with the stars was rare. Galway goalkeeper
Manus Breathnach obliges his fan club after a league defeat to Cavan

(2) Selfie 2. Tipperary's Kieran Bergin is pictured with Ben Mulcare, from Carrick-on-Suir, after
Tipp's win over Kilkenny in Thurles

(3) Selfie 3. The ever obliging Kerry manager Éamonn Fitzmaurice remains true to form as he poses
with Tralee girls Leana O'Shea, Eimear Brosnan and Blathnad Cotter after Kerry beat Donegal

" There are no excuses as regards missing players. There's no point talking about that, it's not an issue. We had players out there, they are all part of the panel **"**

Kilkenny manager Brian Cody is not looking for excuses following a 12-point league defeat to old rivals Tipperary

3.

17 AIB GAA Hurling All-Ireland Senior Club Championship Final - Croke Park, Dublin
Ballyhale Shamrocks 1-18   Kilmallock 1-06

AIB GAA Football All-Ireland Senior Club Championship Final - Croke Park, Dublin
Corofin 1-14   Slaughtneil 0-07

1.

2.

(1) Still going strong – albeit on a different level. James Cha Fitzpatrick gets his shot off, avoiding an attempted hook by Gavin O'Mahony of Kilmallock. The snapshot is indicative of the upper hand enjoyed by Ballyhale Shamrocks in the club hurling final

(2) You never tire of this. Ballyhale's TJ Reid is well on his way to becoming one of the most decorated players of the modern era. The Tommy Moore Cup is the latest addition to his collection

(3) 'I can do this with my eyes closed'. Oddly the player with his eyes shut makes the catch, Daithí Burke of Corofin showing great athleticism to outfield Slaughtneil's Karl McKaigue

(4) The illustrious few. Corofin captain Michael Farragher joins the select few who have collected All-Ireland senior honours as captain after his club's impressive win over Derry and Ulster champions Slaughtneil

" We worked hard on tackling over the last couple of weeks, tackling fairly, giving away as few frees as possible. The lads did that, forced the Kilmallock lads to shoot from distance "

Ballyhale Shamrocks joint manager Andy Moloney on how they secured a record sixth All-Ireland club title

4.

2.

(1) Budding photographer. Newbridge eight-year-old Henry Pipar, Canon camera in hand, is perfectly positioned to capture the action as Tipperary edge Cork by a point in a free-scoring shoot-out

(2) Starting from the ground up. One-year-old Alísha Farrell nails her colours to the mast, inspecting the team photograph benches before Kilkenny's dramatic one-point win over Clare at Nowlan Park

28 Allianz National Hurling League - Croke Park, Dublin
Dublin 1-25   Limerick 0-16

Allianz National Football League - O'Moore Park, Portlaoise
Laois 1-09   Kildare 1-12

Allianz National Football League - Croke Park, Dublin
Dublin 0-08   Derry 0-04

Allianz National Hurling League - O'Moore Park, Portlaoise
Laois 2-18   Antrim 1-13

3.

1.

2.

(1) Runaround in the rain. Limerick's Graeme Mulcahy gets his shot away despite the best efforts of Dublin defender Shane Durkin, but it was not a happy visit to Croke Park for the Munster men

(2) The local ones hurt more. Evan O'Carroll does nothing to hide his disappointment on a night when Laois lose on their own patch to neighbours Kildare

(3) If ever a photograph told the story of a game. Dublin attacker Cormac Costello retains possession in the downpour but the determination etched on the face of Oisín Duffy typifies Derry's approach to the game. Dublin prevail in a game remembered for blanket defences and poor entertainment

(4) It's in there. Somewhere. Laois and Antrim players compete for possession at O'Moore Park before the points go to camp blue and white

4.

" From a defensive point of view we did the business, but until
the GAA authorities do something to change the rules or
whatever, unfortunately that's the way a lot of games are going.
Believe me, it's not the way we want to play football **"**

Derry manager Brian McIver justifies their defensive approach in a low-scoring defeat to Dublin

29 Allianz National Football League - Páirc Uí Rinn, Cork
Cork 2-07   Mayo 0-12

Allianz National Hurling League - Nowlan Park, Kilkenny
Kilkenny 1-18   Clare 1-17

2.

(1) 'Never laid a glove on him ref'. Mayo goalkeeper David Clarke's fingerprints are all over Brian Hurley of Cork on a day when the Rebel campaign is bolstered by two more league points

(2) Kilkenny and a relegation play-off? Clare's Conor McGrath and Shane Prendergast of Kilkenny reach out in the battle for possession on a day when Brian Cody's men record a one-point win to secure top-flight hurling for 2016

29

Allianz National Hurling League - Walsh Park, Waterford
Waterford 0-20   Galway 0-12

Allianz National Football League - MacCumhaill Park, Ballybofey
Donegal 1-13   Tyrone 0-06

Allianz National Football League - Austin Stack Park, Tralee
Kerry 0-10   Monaghan 1-11

Allianz National Hurling League - Páirc Uí Rinn, Cork
Cork 0-18   Wexford 0-14

1.

2.

3.

(1) Ploughing a lonely Walsh Park furrow. Waterford attacker Colin Dunford is engulfed in maroon as Galway trio John Hanbury, Pádraig Mannion and Gearóid McInerney close in. The hosts win pulling up

(2) Two forwards tangling? Modern football. Two of the most respected forwards in the game - Seán Cavanagh in possession and Michael Murphy – come into contact during a Ballybofey league game that goes very much the way of Donegal

(3) Man, ball, the lot. Monaghan goalkeeper Rory Beggan does what's required to keep Kerry substitute Thomas Hickey at bay as Drew Wylie offers support. Monaghan win in Tralee

(4) Someone doing a deal on lime-green hurley grips? The eyes of Cork's Daniel Kearney and Liam Óg McGovern of Wexford are locked on the sliotar as Cork make the most of home advantage

4.

" To come down here and beat fellas that have All-Ireland medals in their back pockets, that's very good for morale "

Monaghan manager Malachy O'Rourke is happy after their first win over Kerry in league or championship since 1988

4

Allianz National Hurling League Division 2B Final - Cusack Park, Mullingar
Kildare 0-22   Meath 0-17

Allianz National Hurling League Division 2A Final - Gaelic Grounds, Limerick
Kerry 5-17   Westmeath 3-17

Allianz National Hurling League Division 3A Final - Keady Lámh Dhearg, Co. Armagh
Tyrone 0-18   Monaghan 1-11

Allianz National Hurling League Division 3B Final - Sean Eiffe Park, Ratoath, Co Meath
Warwickshire 1-15   Longford 2-10

1.

2.

3.

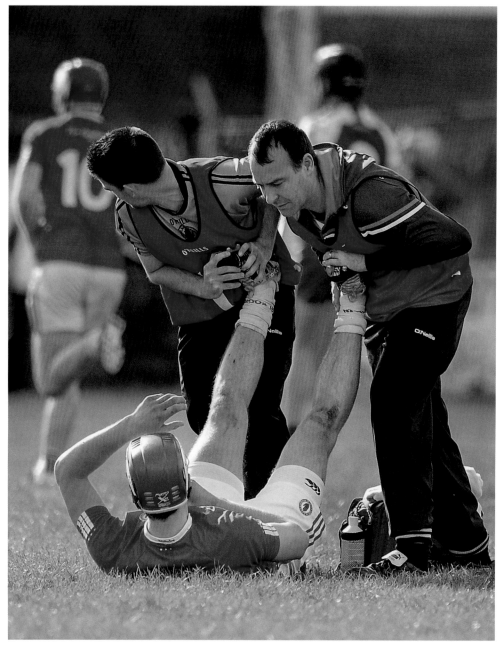

(1) Behind every successful man there stands a woman. Kildare's Division 2B hurling league final win over Meath in Mullingar gives rise to family celebrations as Leo Quinn, Éanna O'Neill and Martin Fitzgerald pose for a photograph with their mothers, Catherine, Mary and Joan, respectively

(2) In for a penny, in for a pound. Kerry's Seán Weir fully commits in his attempt to block Darragh Clinton of Westmeath as the Kingdom hurlers claim Division 2A honours in Limerick

(3) Cramping his style. Tyrone captain Damien Casey is treated for cramp late in his county's Division 3A final win over Monaghan in Keady

(4) Spreading the gospel. Hurling success for the West Midlands as Warwickshire celebrate their Division 3B league final win over Longford in Ratoath

4.

5 Allianz National Football League - Healy Park, Omagh
Tyrone 0-17 Kerry 1-14

Allianz National Football League - St. Tiernach's Park, Clones
Monaghan 1-11 Dublin 1-22

Allianz National Football League - Owenbeg, Derry
Derry 2-15 Cork 1-11

Allianz National Football League - Páirc Esler, Newry
Down 3-12 Laois 1-15

1.

2.

(1) Return of the Great One. Colm Cooper reaches to shake Bryan Sheehan's hand as he makes his way on to the field in a Kerry jersey for the first time since the 2013 All-Ireland semi-final. A cruciate ligament injury kept Cooper sidelined, and his return coincides with Tyrone's relegation to Division Two

(2) Toe curled and in full flight. Darren Hughes of Monaghan solos the ball in Clones as Dublin's Michael Darragh Macauley senses the danger. Dublin win well on their travels

(3) Chest high. Derry's Liam McGoldrick holds on to the ball despite a tackle by Mark Collins of Cork during a comfortable win for the home team in Owenbeg

(4) Hard to salvage much from that one. Ross Munnelly cuts a dejected figure

4.

5 Allianz National Football League - County Grounds, Drogheda
Louth 2-11   Limerick 2-13

Allianz National Football League - Elverys MacHale Park, Castlebar
Mayo 0-12   Donegal 1-09

Allianz National Football League - Páirc Tailteann, Navan
Meath 0-14   Cavan 0-12

1.

2.

(1) 'I make that six'. Louth manager Colin Kelly takes a time-check late on in a home defeat to Limerick

(2) Heels over head. Donegal's Karl Lacey takes a tumble under pressure from Aidan O'Shea of Mayo as the counties take a point each from their Castlebar clash

(3) Plenty to ponder. Meath's Conor Gillespie, whose 2014 season was ruined by a cruciate ligament injury, is in reflective mood as he waits alone to speak to the print media following his team's win over Cavan in Navan

3.

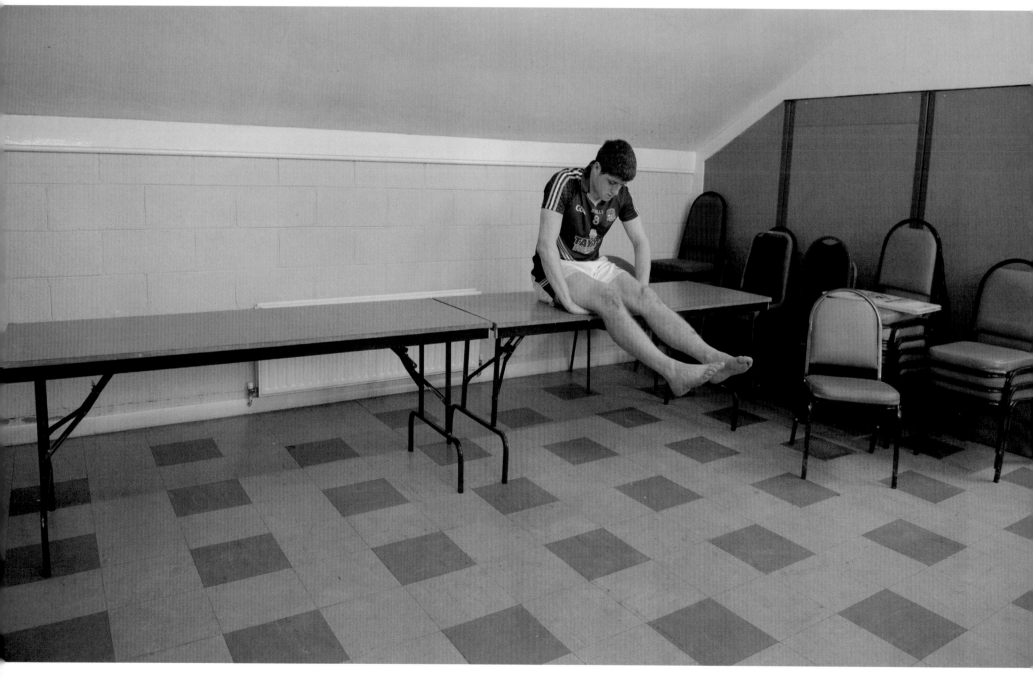

11 Allianz National Hurling League Division 1B Promotion / Relegation Play-off - Parnell Park, Dublin
Kerry 2-16   Antrim 1-18

12 Allianz National Hurling League Division 2B Promotion / Relegation Play-off - Owenbeg, Derry
Donegal 4-13   Tyrone 4-13

Allianz National Football League Division 1 Semi-Final - Croke Park, Dublin
Dublin 0-17   Monaghan 0-16

Allianz National Football League Division 1 Semi-Final - Croke Park, Dublin
Cork 4-11   Donegal 0-19

1.

2.

3.

4.

(1) Toned and tattooed. Adrian Royle leads the post-match sing-song after Kerry's hurlers seal promotion following a play-off win over Antrim at Parnell Park

(2) Low division, high skills. Tyrone's Damien Casey leads the charge against Jamesie Donnelly of Donegal as the counties draw in a Division 2B play-off in Owenbeg

(3) Punctuality is the soul of business. GAA director general Páraic Duffy takes his seat early for the National League semi-final between his native Monaghan and defending champions Dublin – their second encounter in a week. Dublin prevail again, but only just on this occasion

(4) Job done and smiles of satisfaction. Cork goalkeeper Ken O'Halloran and Barry O'Driscoll enjoy the moment after they defeated Donegal and booked their place in the National League final

18 EirGrid GAA Football All-Ireland Under 21 Championship Semi-Final - O'Connor Park, Tullamore
Tipperary 0-14   Dublin 0-12

19 Allianz National Hurling League Division 1 Semi-Final - Nowlan Park, Kilkenny
Cork 1-27   Dublin 2-23

Allianz National Hurling League Division 1 Semi-Final - Nowlan Park, Kilkenny
Waterford 1-19   Tipperary 2-15

" I don't like doing it too often. You can't be giving yourself big leads to peg back like that. But I thought our lads grew in confidence and just about deserved it, probably lucky to win in fairness "

Cork manager Jimmy Barry Murphy is a relieved man after his team clawed back
a 12-point deficit against Dublin in the league semi-final

1.

2.

3.

(1) A measure of the man. Five footballers in sky blue jerseys join four in blue and gold – all connected with UCD – to remember the GAA giant that was Dave Billings before the Dublin-Tipperary All-Ireland under-21 semi-final in Tullamore

(2) Championship-style celebrations. Cork hurling manager Jimmy Barry Murphy is particularly animated after a league semi-final win over Dublin in Nowlan Park. A stunning comeback lies behind his glee

(3) Easy does it. Pauric Mahony strokes over the winning point in Waterford's league semi-final success over Tipperary in Kilkenny

25 Allianz National Football League Division 3, Final - Croke Park, Dublin
Armagh 0-16 Fermanagh 0-11

Allianz National Football League Division 2 Final - Croke Park, Dublin
Roscommon 1-17 Down 0-15

26 Allianz National Football League Division 4 Final - Croke Park, Dublin
Offaly 4-16 Longford 1-12

Allianz National Football League Division 1 Final - Croke Park, Dublin
Dublin 1-21 Cork 2-07

1.

2.

3.

4.

(1) All light and happiness. Armagh players pose – almost perfectly – for the winners'
team shot after their Division Three league final win over Fermanagh at Croke Park

(2) Happy Rossies. The full Roscommon complement get in on the celebratory act
following their Division Two league final success over Down

(3) Up she flew. Offaly captain Paul McConway hoists the fruits of his team's work as
they beat Longford in the Division Four league decider

(4) Familiar sight? The Dublin footballers celebrate their third consecutive league
crown after a comprehensive victory over Cork in Croke Park

2 EirGrid GAA Football All-Ireland Under 21 Championship Final - Parnell Park, Dublin
Tyrone 1-11   Tipperary 0-13

3 Leinster GAA Hurling Senior Championship Round Robin - Ballycastle, Co. Antrim
Antrim 5-17   Laois 3-22

Leinster GAA Hurling Senior Championship Round Robin - Cusack Park, Mullingar
Westmeath 2-19   Carlow 2-17

Connacht GAA Football Senior Championship - Gaelic Park, New York
New York 0-08   Galway 2-18

2.

3.

4.

(1) The bumps for the boss. Manager Feargal Logan is thrown airborne after Tyrone's All-Ireland under-21 final win over Tipperary at Parnell Park. The second half was delayed because two spectators suffered heart attacks

(2) Laois hung out to dry? Letters dangle mid-air as officials adjust the scoreboard ahead of the Antrim-Laois Leinster championship match in Ballycastle. An injury-time goal denies the visitors

(3) 'C'mere to me lads'. Westmeath hurling manager Michael Ryan embraces Niall O'Brien, left, and Aonghus Clarke after their win over Carlow

(4) No fairytale in New York. Galway's Damien Comer is tackled by Gerard McCartan in Gaelic Park as the Connacht championship gets lift-off with a maroon win in the Big Apple

3 Allianz National Hurling League Division 1 Final - Semple Stadium, Thurles
Waterford 1-24   Cork 0-17

1.

2.

(1) Rising tide. Waterford captain Kevin Moran has something
tangible to show for his team's progress as National League
honours are secured against Cork in Thurles

(2) Déise delight. Waterford supporters stream on to the
Thurles turf for the presentation of the league trophy

" No one does lying in the grass better than Cork and that's what they'll be doing for the next five weeks "

Waterford manager Derek McGrath is not taking the championship clash against
Cork for granted despite beating the Rebels in the league final

10 Leinster GAA Hurling Senior Championship Round Robin - Cusack Park, Mullingar
Westmeath 1-21   Antrim 0-07

16 Leinster GAA Football Senior Championship - O'Connor Park, Tullamore
Offaly 0-13   Longford 0-16

Leinster GAA Football Senior Championship - Netwatch Dr. Cullen Park, Carlow
Carlow 0-08   Laois 3-16

1.

2.

(1) Upsetting the applecart. Westmeath manager Michael Ryan
fuels up on the go as he sees his team give Antrim the runaround
in Cusack Park

(2) Testing the faith of the Faithful. Offaly supporter Michael
McDonagh, from Tullamore, experiences despair – and worse –
at O'Connor Park as he witnesses his team's loss to Longford
in the Leinster football championship

(3) A little popper. Laois forward Donie Kingston lets a pass off
despite the best efforts of Seán Gannon and Shane Redmond of
Carlow. Laois win comfortably

3.

1.

2.

3.

❝ The demise of Gaelic football has been exaggerated **❞**

RTÉ analyst Colm O'Rourke after the Ulster championship game between
Donegal and Tyrone in Ballybofey

17 Connacht GAA Football Senior Championship - Páirc Seán Mac Diarmada, Carrick-on-Shannon
Leitrim 0-08   Galway 1-13

Ulster GAA Football Senior Championship - MacCumhaill Park, Ballybofey
Donegal 1-13   Tyrone 1-10

23 Munster GAA Football Senior Championship - Cusack Park, Ennis
Clare 0-15   Limerick 0-13

24 Ulster GAA Football Senior Championship - Kingspan Breffni Park, Cavan
Cavan 0-15   Monaghan 0-16

Connacht GAA Football Senior Championship - Páirc Smárgaid, Ruislip, London
London 0-10   Roscommon 1-14

4.

5.

(1) Full blooded. Damien Comer of Galway mixes it with Leitrim goalkeeper Cathal McCrann and full back Ronan Gallagher. Galway emerge from Carrick-on-Shannon intact

(2) Me and my shadow. A familiar snapshot from Donegal's opening-round match against Tyrone at Ballybofey as Justin McMahon gets touch tight with Michael Murphy. It only partially works as the hosts navigate a potential derailment

(3) Elevated position. Clare manager Colm Collins, serving a suspension, follows his team's clash with Limerick from a gantry with a steward close by. Clare come out tops

(4) Job done. Just. Colin Walshe celebrates after scoring Monaghan's last score in a one-point win over Cavan. Coming after a long absence through injury makes it all the sweeter for Walshe

(5) The Exile. Steward Tom O'Connor, living in London 55 years and originally from Newcastle West in Limerick, monitors the Roscommon footballers as they make their way to the dressingroom at Ruislip. The visitors would prove too strong

MAY '15

24   Leinster GAA Hurling Senior Championship Round Robin - Netwatch Dr. Cullen Park, Carlow
Carlow 2-18   Antrim 1-11

Munster GAA Hurling Senior Championship - Semple Stadium, Thurles
Limerick 1-19   Clare 2-15

31   Ulster GAA Football Senior Championship - Brewster Park, Enniskillen
Fermanagh 1-13   Antrim 0-08

1.

2.

(1)   Red is the colour. And green. And yellow. Carlow-coloured seats in the main stand at Dr Cullen Park provide the backdrop for manager Pat English's post-match talk as Carlow see off the Antrim challenge

(2)   Floating on air. Limerick's Cian Lynch and Domhnall O'Donovan of Clare find it hard to stay grounded as they eye the sliotar during their Munster championship clash in Thurles. Limerick scrape through

(3)   Not letting go. Antrim's Conor Burke keeps his eye on the ball as he and Seán Quigley from Fermanagh jostle for possession at Brewster Park. The hosts avenge defeat to the same opposition at the same venue a year earlier

" You always have nerves before a game. Without nerves there is no point playing, but it's good nerves **"**

Limerick forward Cian Lynch after an impressive Munster championship debut against Clare

3.

31 Leinster GAA Hurling Senior Championship - Croke Park, Dublin
Dublin 0-20   Galway 1-17

Leinster GAA Football Senior Championship - Croke Park, Dublin
Dublin 4-25   Longford 0-10

Munster GAA Football Senior Championship - Semple Stadium, Thurles
Tipperary 1-24   Waterford 0-05

1.

2.

(1) 'Right here'. Croke Park umpire Johnny Fitzpatrick indicates to the referee that the sliotar struck the helmet of a Dublin player and a 65 should be awarded. The Dubs and Galway play out a draw

(2) Up and running. Goalscorer Diarmuid Connolly accepts the congratulations of team-mate Bernard Brogan, left, as the umpire reaches for green. There is not much Paddy McCollum can do in the Longford goal

(3) Within reach. Waterford's Patrick Hurney tries to get two hands on the ball just ahead of Steven O'Brien of Tipperary in Thurles. The hosts have 22 points to spare

3.

6

Nicky Rackard Cup Final - Croke Park, Dublin
Roscommon 2-12 Armagh 1-14

Lory Meagher Cup Final - Croke Park, Dublin
Fermanagh 3-16 Sligo 1-17

Christy Ring Cup Final - Croke Park, Dublin
Kerry 1-20 Derry 0-12

Leinster GAA Football Senior Championship - O'Connor Park, Tullamore
Kildare 0-16 Laois 0-16

Leinster GAA Hurling Senior Championship - O'Connor Park, Tullamore
Galway 5-19 Dublin 1-18

1.

2.

3.

4.

(1-3) Nobody does it better. Croke Park is synonymous with victorious team pictures as Roscommon, Fermanagh and Kerry get in on the act after Nicky Rackard, Lory Meagher and Christy Ring Cup final wins over Armagh, Sligo and Derry, respectively

(4) Turning a blind eye? Paul Cribben of Kildare feels the full force of two Laois tackles as Evan O'Carroll, left, and Damien O'Connor get up close and personal. It's as tight on the scoreboard as the teams play out a draw

(5) Hand to eye co-ordination. Chris Crummy of Dublin attempts to grab the sliotar as Galway's Joe Canning waits for it to drop. Galway blitz Dublin in their Leinster replay in Tullamore

1.

7 Munster GAA Hurling Senior Championship - Semple Stadium, Thurles
Waterford 3-19   Cork 1-21

Ulster GAA Football Senior Championship - Celtic Park, Derry
Derry 0-12   Down 0-11

2.

(1) Still fine-tuning. Waterford manager Derek McGrath
continues to issue instructions, even as his charges
prepare for the pre-match photo ahead of their Munster
assignment against Cork. It works

(2) Climb any mountain. Eoin Bradley and Seán Leo
McGoldrick ascend the Celtic Park steps ahead of a
successful Ulster outing against Down

7 Leinster GAA Hurling Senior Championship - O'Moore Park, Portlaoise
Laois 0-29   Offaly 0-21

13 Leinster GAA Football Senior Championship Replay - O'Connor Park, Tullamore
Kildare 3-18   Laois 1-11

14 Ulster GAA Football Senior Championship - Athletic Grounds, Armagh
Armagh 0-08   Donegal 2-11

Munster GAA Football Senior Championship - Semple Stadium, Thurles
Tipperary 2-08   Kerry 2-14

1.

2.

(1) Respectful handshake. Offaly hurling manager Brian Whelahan is quite downbeat as he congratulates his counterpart Séamus Plunkett after Laois's breakthrough success over their illustrious neighbours

(2) Dapper réiteoir. Referee Anthony Nolan inspects the hardware in his Sunday best before swapping grey for black for the Kildare-Laois replay at O'Connor Park

(3) 'Yesssssss!' Paddy McBrearty doesn't attempt to hide his delight after striking for Donegal's first goal in an impressive away win over Armagh

(4) Living legend. Kerry great Mick O'Dwyer takes time out to chew the fat with Thurles stadium director David Morgan before the Kingdom's win over Tipperary

4.

14 Leinster GAA Football Senior Championship - Cusack Park, Mullingar
Westmeath 1-21   Wexford 0-15

Leinster GAA Football Senior Championship - Páirc Tailteann, Navan
Meath 2-19   Wicklow 3-12

Connacht GAA Football Senior Championship - Pearse Stadium, Salthill
Galway 2-08   Mayo 1-15

Munster GAA Football Senior Championship - Páirc Uí Rinn, Cork
Cork 1-20   Clare 1-08

1.

2.

3.

(1) Easy up. Joey Wadding of Wexford vaults over Westmeath's Kieran Martin in Mullingar before the hosts book a ticket to the next stage of what would become a memorable campaign

(2) Anticipating the breaking ball. Meath trio, from left, James McEntee, Adam Flanagan and Nicky Judge jostle for possession with the Wicklow duo of John McGrath and Stephen Kelly in Navan. The hosts see it out after getting a scare

(3) 'We're behind you'. Galway get a view of their Mayo counterparts on the big screen at Pearse Stadium during Amhrán na bhFiann. Galway v Mayo by the seaside means that summer, or our equivalent of it, has arrived

(4) Holding on. Clare midfielder Gary Brennan keeps possession as Cork's Alan O'Connor, left, and Kevin O'Driscoll close in at Páirc Uí Rinn. There are no shocks in this one

4.

❝ It was all about getting the win. We didn't play particularly well in a lot of aspects of the game but in fairness to the lads, they all kept plugging away and kept working hard and we got the result in the end ❞

Joint manager Pat Holmes after his Mayo team extended their championship winning streak to five in a row over arch rivals Galway

20 GAA Football All-Ireland Senior Championship Qualifiers, Round 1A - Páirc Smárgaid, Ruislip, London
London 0-11   Cavan 2-22

GAA Football All-Ireland Senior Championship Qualifiers, Round 1A - Glennon Brothers Pearse Park, Longford
Longford 2-15   Carlow 1-08

GAA Football All-Ireland Senior Championship Qualifiers, Round 1A - O'Moore Park, Portlaoise
Laois 1-16   Antrim 2-15

1.

2.

(1) Roadblock for an old friend. Cavan native Lorcan Mulvey, now starring for London, is apprehended by Jason McLoughlin and Martin Reilly in Ruislip. Cavan end London's summer

(2) Protocols. Longford's John Geelan raises the Tricolour in Pearse Park before a comfortable qualifier win for the home team over Carlow

(3) Colour-coded elation and despair. Laois are left with the blues while the Saffrons celebrate after Patrick McBride, left, scores a late point in Antrim's sensational win in Portlaoise

" It wasn't easy because the three lads have been very loyal to us all year. It was just one of those things that had to be dealt with. I spoke to the players and they understood **"**

Antrim manager Frank Fitzsimons on the tough decision to drop three of his players for the Laois game because they had played a hurling match the previous night

3.

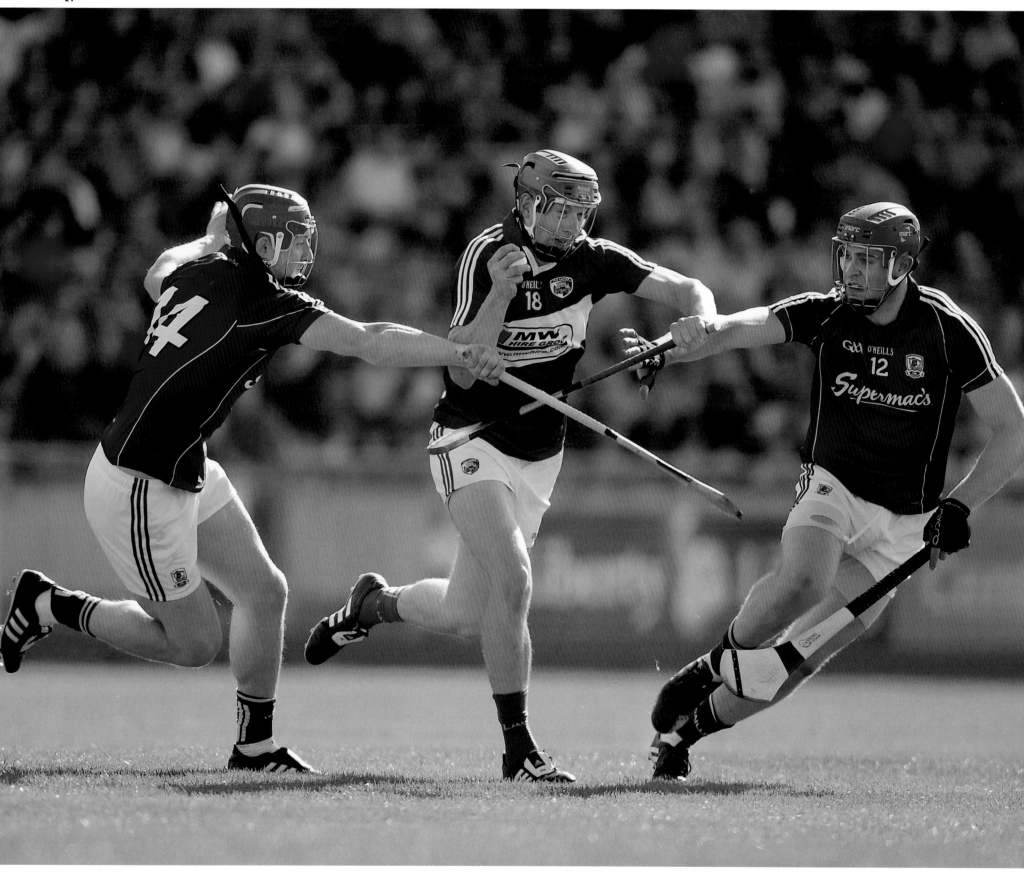

20 Leinster GAA Hurling Senior Championship - O'Connor Park, Tullamore
Galway 3-28 Laois 1-14

Connacht GAA Football Senior Championship - Markievicz Park, Sligo
Sligo 1-14 Roscommon 0-13

2.

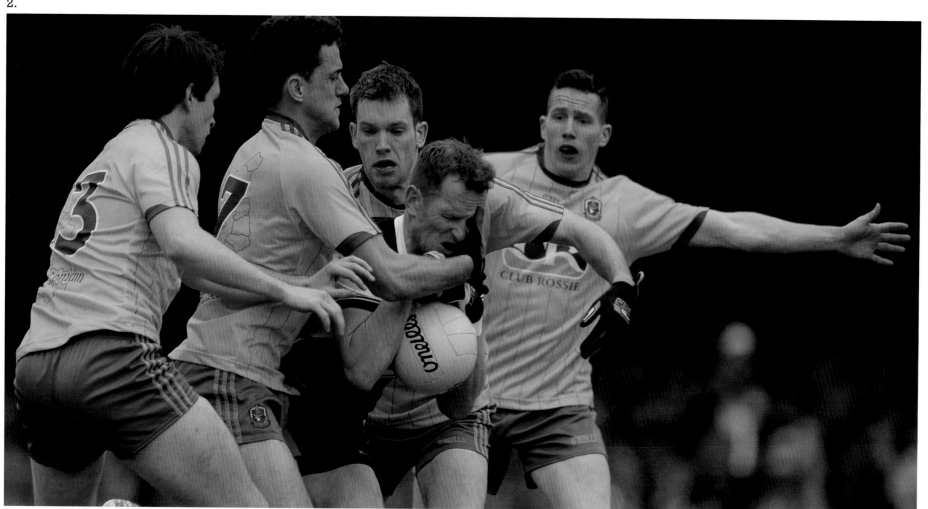

(1) Power surge. Stephen Maher of Laois bursts forward against Galway
in Tullamore but Joe Canning, left, and Jonathan Glynn are on hand to
halt his gallop – and prevent any more heroics from Laois

(2) Lemon squash. Mark Brehony runs into Roscommon traffic in the
shape of, from left, David Keenan, Ciarán Cafferky, Niall Carty and
Seán McDermott. Sligo pull off a memorable win

21 Leinster GAA Hurling Senior Championship - Nowlan Park, Kilkenny
Kilkenny 5-25   Wexford 0-16

Munster GAA Hurling Senior Championship - Gaelic Grounds, Limerick
Limerick 1-16   Tipperary 4-23

Ulster GAA Hurling Senior Championship - Athletic Grounds, Armagh
Armagh 3-14   Down 5-20

1.

2.

(1) Referees have calf muscles too. Diarmuid Kirwan requires the attention of Kilkenny team doctor Tadhg Crowley during the home side's easier than expected victory over Wexford at Nowlan Park

(2) Full on. Séamus Callanan's teeth shatter after a clash of helmets and face guards with Limerick goalkeeper Barry Hennessy at the Gaelic Grounds. The Tipperary man was bleeding profusely but returned to the field after treatment

(3) It didn't go our way. A young supporter, hurley in hand, sheds a tear after Armagh's Ulster championship reversal to Down at the Athletic Grounds

3

21 Ulster GAA Football Senior Championship - Kingspan Breffni Park, Cavan
Monaghan 1-20   Fermanagh 0-13

27 Ulster GAA Football Senior Championship - St Tiernach's Park, Clones
Donegal 1-09   Derry 0-10

1.

(1) Firmly rooted. One of the stars of the championship, Conor McManus, embraces Laura Finlay, from Ballybay, following Monaghan's Ulster win over Fermanagh in Cavan

(2) A bit of light reading. Donegal midfielder Neil Gallagher studies the match programme while on the treatment table before his team's successful Clones test against Derry

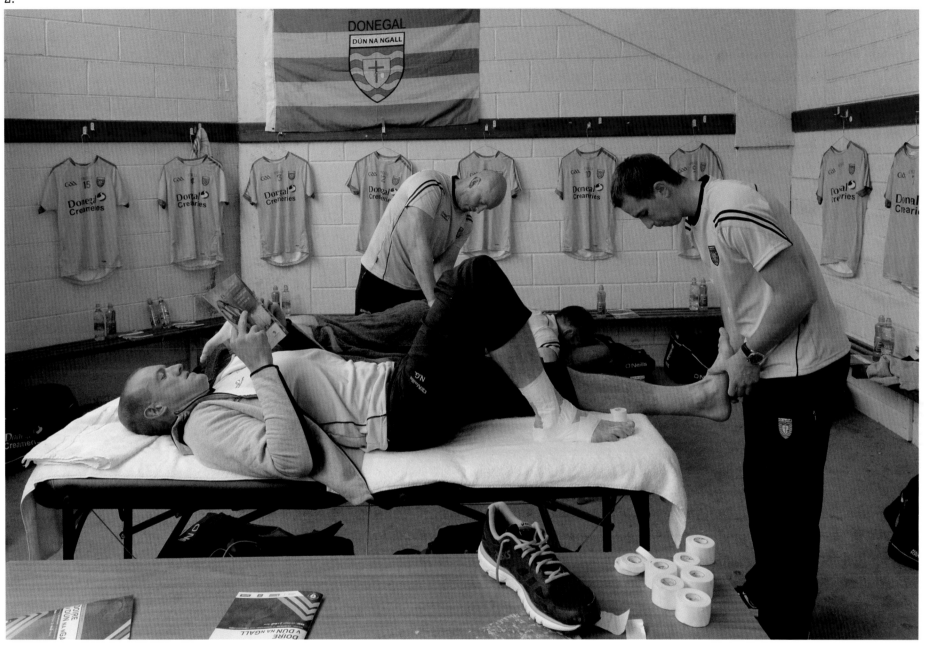

" We left this game behind us. We fully believed we were going to win this game; we prepared really well and created chances "

A disappointed Derry manager Brian McIver after their Ulster semi-final defeat to Donegal

27 GAA Football All-Ireland Senior Championship, Qualifiers: Round 1B - Athletic Grounds, Armagh
Armagh 2-17   Wicklow 2-07

GAA Football All-Ireland Senior Championship, Qualifiers: Round 1B - County Grounds, Drogheda
Louth 1-16   Leitrim 0-11

GAA Football All-Ireland Senior Championship, Qualifiers: Round 1B - Innovate Wexford Park, Wexford
Wexford 2-16   Down 2-11

28 Leinster GAA Football Senior Championship - Croke Park, Dublin
Westmeath 3-19   Meath 2-18

1.

2.

3.

(1) Put it there. Armagh manager Kieran McGeeney shakes hands with his seven-year-old son Cian after their qualifier win over Wicklow at the Athletic Grounds

(2) A job to be done after the job is done. Conor McGinty, aged nine and from Drogheda, takes a goal net from the field after Louth end Leitrim's summer

(3) That winning feeling. Wexford football manager David Power rejoices with confirmation of a win over Down, his first senior championship success

(4) Westmeath go wild 1. Ray Connellan celebrates one of the comebacks of the summer as Westmeath record their first win over Meath in championship football

(5) Westmeath go wild 2. The faces of the Westmeath supporters convey the emotions of the day. They have just seen their team come back from the dead to floor the county that has caused them more heartbreak than any other

5.

❝ We didn't expect to be down that much at half-time. We had a lot of lads who had never played senior championship football at Croke Park before and there were a few nerves in the first half. It's a great feeling to get our first ever win in the championship against Meath, and to do it that way is even better **❞**

Westmeath's Kieran Martin after their incredible second-half comeback in the Leinster semi-final

1.

28 Leinster GAA Football Senior Championship - Croke Park, Dublin
Dublin 5-18   Kildare 0-14

GAA Football All-Ireland Senior Championship, Qualifiers: Round 1B - Healy Park, Omagh
Tyrone 1-14   Limerick 0-08

4 GAA Football All-Ireland Senior Championship, Qualifiers: Round 2A - Cusack Park, Ennis
Clare 1-12   Longford 2-12

2.

3.

(1) Paying their respects. Supporters on Hill 16 honour brothers Alan and Stephen Harris – two Dublin fans who lost their lives in a tragic accident in Portmarnock – and also the victims of the Berkeley disaster in California, with sustained applause in the 16th minute of the game against Kildare

(2) Checkpoint. Tom Lee of Limerick is held up by Tyrone's Aidan McCrory in the counties' qualifier in Omagh

(3) Another scalp on the road. Longford manager Jack Sheedy is jubilant after seeing the Midlanders follow up their away win over Offaly by defeating Clare in Ennis

4

GAA Football All-Ireland Senior Championship, Qualifiers: Round 2A - O'Connor Park, Tullamore
Offaly 1-13 Kildare 1-15

GAA Hurling All-Ireland Senior Championship, Qualifiers: Round 1 - O'Moore Park, Portlaoise
Laois 0-19 Dublin 4-17

GAA Hurling All-Ireland Senior Championship, Qualifiers: Round 1 - Innovate Wexford Park, Wexford
Wexford 0-20 Cork 2-22

GAA Hurling All-Ireland Senior Championship, Qualifiers: Round 1 - Cusack Park, Ennis
Clare 3-26 Offaly 0-15

GAA Football All-Ireland Senior Championship, Qualifiers: Round 2A - Kingspan Breffni Park, Cavan
Cavan 1-16 Roscommon 3-17

3.

1.

2.

4.

5.

(1) The end of the road. Offaly's Joseph O'Connor reacts to his team's defeat to Kildare in Tullamore

(2) A shoulder to lean on. Laois manager Séamus Plunkett consoles corner back Brian Stapleton after they crash out against Dublin

(3) That's the one. Conor Lehane celebrates his goal for Cork in a win away against Wexford

(4) The sideline can be a lonely place. Offaly manager Brian Whelahan, one of the all-time great hurlers, seems weighed down by the demands of management. Clare call time on Offaly's season – and Whelahan's tenure

(5) Class in defeat. Cavan manager Terry Hyland congratulates his Roscommon counterpart John Evans during an interview. The man with the mic is Billy Joe Padden of Newstalk

5
GAA Hurling All-Ireland Senior Championship, Qualifiers: Round 1- Cusack Park, Mullingar
Westmeath 1-12 Limerick 4-15

GAA Football All-Ireland Senior Championship Qualifiers: Round 2A - Brewster Park, Enniskillen
Fermanagh 1-21 Antrim 0-11

6.

7.

" We all know how talented he is and he will realise that when you score 14 points you've got to be ready for a bit more attention next time **"**

Fermanagh manager Pete McGrath on his young star Seán Quigley

(6) Umbrellas in the stand. A testing Irish summer produces a wet day for the good folk in Mullingar. Limerick keep the home challenge at arm's length

(7) Taking it all in. Antrim's Mark Sweeney digests the qualifier reversal against Fermanagh

5 Leinster GAA Hurling Senior Championship Final - Croke Park, Dublin
Kilkenny 1-25   Galway 2-15

Munster GAA Football Senior Championship Final - Fitzgerald Stadium, Killarney
Kerry 2-15   Cork 3-12

11 GAA Football All-Ireland Senior Championship, Qualifiers: Round 2B - Owenbeg, Dungiven
Derry 1-16   Wexford 0-10

GAA Football All-Ireland Senior Championship, Qualifiers: Round 2B - Healy Park, Omagh
Tyrone 1-10   Meath 0-11

2.

3.

4.

(1) Controlled jubilation. Even in the company of silverware you get the feeling that there are bigger fish on the horizon for the Kilkenny hurlers. Nevertheless they're enjoying their latest Leinster final win, this time over Galway

(2) 'You've got to be kidding ref'. Mark Collins of Cork, third from right, reacts with utter disbelief to referee Pádraig Hughes's decision to award Kerry a penalty in the counties' Munster final draw

(3) In a state of readiness. Derry's Chrissy McKaigue is on the front foot against Adrian Flynn of Wexford

(4) Encouraging the next generation. Tyrone manager Mickey Harte poses for a picture with young supporters after the county's win over Meath in Omagh

11   GAA Football All-Ireland Senior Championship, Qualifiers: Round 2B - Semple Stadium, Thurles
Tipperary 3-21   **Louth 0-07**

GAA Hurling All-Ireland Senior Championship, Qualifiers: Round 2 - Semple Stadium, Thurles
Dublin 1-17   **Limerick 1-16**

GAA Football All-Ireland Senior Championship, Qualifiers: Round 3A - Cusack Park, Mullingar
Longford 0-11   **Kildare 2-24**

1.

3.

(1) The classic block. Louth's Pádraig Rath gets both hands out to block the shot of Ger Mulhair of Tipperary in Thurles. Otherwise it was all downhill for the men in red

(2) Relief or jubilation? Dublin's Johnny McCaffrey drops to his knees on the final whistle as a one-point qualifier win is confirmed against Limerick in Thurles

(3) 'If you're going down, I'm going too'. Niall Kelly of Kildare battles with Colm Smyth of Longford as the Lilywhites turn the screw to win with plenty to spare

11   GAA Hurling All-Ireland Senior Championship, Qualifiers: Round 2 - Semple Stadium, Thurles
Clare 0-17   Cork 0-20

Ulster GAA Hurling Senior Championship Final - Owenbeg, Dungiven
Antrim 1-15   Down 1-14

12   Leinster GAA Football Senior Championship Final - Croke Park, Dublin
Dublin 2-13   Westmeath 0-06

1.

2.

3.

(1)   That one hurt. Clare's Conor Ryan reacts to defeat by Cork in Thurles.
It's a year-ending loss for the Banner

(2)   A mix of experience … and youth. Children gatecrash the party as
Antrim bookend a disappointing year with a one-point win over Down
in the Ulster final at Owenbeg

(3)   This will do nicely … for now. Captain Stephen Cluxton raises the
Delaney Cup after Dublin's Leinster final win over Westmeath at Croke
Park. There are no more maroon miracles

12   GAA Football All-Ireland Senior Championship, Qualifiers: Round 2B - Athletic Grounds, Armagh
Armagh 0-12   Galway 1-12

Munster GAA Hurling Senior Championship Final - Semple Stadium, Thurles
Tipperary 0-21   Waterford 0-16

1.

2.

(1)   Tangerine crusher. Damien Comer, left, celebrates with Galway team-mate Michael Lundy after scoring his team's vital goal against Armagh. It helps Galway to a noteworthy away win

(2)   Calm and composed. Tipperary captain Brendan Maher does the needful after his county's Munster hurling final win over Waterford at Semple Stadium

(3)   Defeat is a lonely place. Patrick Curran seems oblivious to the Tipperary invasion in the immediate aftermath of Waterford's Munster final defeat in Thurles. Tipp captain Brendan Maher and Darren Gleeson spot him as they try to make their way through the crowd

3.

JULY '15

18 GAA Football All-Ireland Senior Championship, Qualifiers: Round 3B - Semple Stadium, Thurles
Tipperary 0-07 Tyrone 0-19

GAA Football All-Ireland Senior Championship, Qualifiers: Round 3B - Pearse Stadium, Salthill
Galway 1-11 Derry 0-08

Munster GAA Football Senior Championship Final Replay - Fitzgerald Stadium, Killarney
Kerry 1-11 Cork 1-06

1.

2.

" Maybe things don't come as easy as they once did, that you have to work that little bit harder for them and that's fine. But it's a lot less frustrating to where I was this time last year "

Kerry's Colm Cooper on his struggle to get back to full fitness after being out injured for over a year

(1) Field of Legends is what it says, and who are we to dispute that assertion when Seán Cavanagh makes his entrance? Tyrone's footballers get a rare chance to parade their skills at 'the home of hurling'

(2) A day of frustration. Derry boss Brian McIver has a bemused air as his team crash out of the championship against Galway on a soft Salthill day. It marks the end of his tenure

(3) A ray of light on a dank day. Kerry captain Kieran Donaghy and GAA president Aogán Ó Fearghail are lit up in the post-match photography frenzy of a Munster final. Kerry learn their lessons from the first day to leave Cork ruing a missed opportunity

1.

2.

(1) Just the three of us. The Gallogly family, Stephen, Caroline and daughter Eva, enjoy a family moment after Monaghan's Anglo-Celt Cup success over Donegal

(2) Sombreros and high fives. Captain Keith Higgins is swamped by Mayo supporters celebrating the county's fifth Connacht title in a row after a massive 26-point win over Sligo at Dr Hyde Park

25 GAA Football All-Ireland Senior Championship, Qualifiers: Round 4A - Kingspan Breffni Park, Cavan
Westmeath 0-07   Fermanagh 1-13

GAA Football All-Ireland Senior Championship, Qualifiers: Round 4A - Semple Stadium, Thurles
Cork 1-13   Kildare 1-21

1.

2.

(1) The long arm of the law. Fermanagh manager Pete McGrath celebrates a qualifier win
over Westmeath with Garda Joe O'Connor in Cavan. Westmeath fail to sparkle after their
Leinster final setback

(2) Blade runner? He covered every blade as a player but on this Saturday evening he's
tending to it on wheels. Former Tipperary hurler Pa Bourke prepares the Semple Stadium
pitch for the next day's triple-header following Kildare's shock qualifier victory over Cork

26 GAA Hurling All-Ireland Senior Championship, Quarter-Final - Semple Stadium, Thurles
Waterford 2-21   Dublin 1-19

GAA Hurling All-Ireland Senior Championship, Quarter-Final - Semple Stadium, Thurles
Galway 2-28   Cork 0-22

(1) Raining on their parade. Hurling quarter-final spectators are caught in a downpour before the meeting of Waterford and Dublin in Thurles

(2) Checking Section 122 of the Act. Gardaí fill out their paperwork in the stand at Semple Stadium after Galway's quarter-final win over Cork brings the curtain down on another busy Sunday

1.

2.

" They know as much about serious-level sport as I do about the sleeping habits of the Ayatollah "

Former Cork goalkeeper and *Sunday Game* analyst Donal Óg Cusack has a cut at Cork's top officials

117

1   GAA Football All-Ireland Senior Championship Qualifiers: Round 4B - Croke Park, Dublin
Tyrone 0-21   Sligo 0-14

GAA Football All-Ireland Senior Championship Qualifiers: Round 4B - Croke Park, Dublin
Donegal 3-12   Galway 0-11

1.

(1) Small steps, big steps. Tyrone defender Joe McMahon is accompanied from the Croke Park field by his three-year-old daughter Aoibhe following Tyrone's win over Sligo

(2) He who hesitates is lost. The Galway panel seem unsure of their next move after the pre-match photograph. When the action begins Donegal prove to be a more formidable challenge than Armagh or Derry, and Galway bow out

❝ I'm not on Twitter so I'm not responsible for what's on that. Michael wasn't injured coming into the game. It was a very unfounded rumour **❞**

Donegal manager Rory Gallagher on the pre-match hearsay surrounding Michael Murphy's fitness. True to form the big Glenswilly man put on a 'man-of-the-match' display against Galway in their qualifier game

2.

" I didn't realise you could tackle the goalkeeper in Gaelic football "

Dublin manager Jim Gavin comments on Fermanagh's controversial goal in the All-Ireland quarter-final

(1)   Well and truly back. Kerry's Colm Cooper leaves the field after Kildare have been dismantled. Gooch shows some of the old magic, scoring two of Kerry's seven goals

(2)   'What are you doing with that?' Stephen Cluxton begs to differ with umpire John Mike Fitzgerald's decision to award a goal after the Dublin goalkeeper was adjudged to have crossed his own line with the ball in the win over Fermanagh

8 GAA Football All-Ireland Senior Championship Quarter-Final - Croke Park, Dublin
Tyrone 0-18   Monaghan 0-14

GAA Football All-Ireland Senior Championship Quarter-Final - Croke Park, Dublin
Mayo 2-13   Donegal 0-11

9 GAA Hurling All-Ireland Senior Championship Semi-Final - Croke Park, Dublin
Kilkenny 1-21   Waterford 0-18

1.

2.

" There has been a bit of talk that I have been only doing it against lesser opposition. Other players around the place are doing it against better opposition. I can do it any day. It doesn't matter who we're playing **"**

Mayo's Aidan O'Shea after an impressive performance at full-forward in the All-Ireland quarter-final against Donegal

4.

(1) Deja vú. Another All-Ireland quarter-final, another defeat for Monaghan veteran Dick Clerkin. This time Tyrone halt the Ulster champions' run, and it seems the favourites' tag doesn't rest easy with them

(2) The Wild West way. Mayo's Aidan O'Shea celebrates his exquisite goal against Donegal at Croke Park. Talk of his Connacht final exhibition of full-forward play being a flash in the pan is buried

(3) That looks like a Kilkenny hand on the sliotar. TJ Reid has the keenest eye amid the swinging hurleys as he and team-mate Ger Aylward tangle for possession with Waterford's Stephen O'Keeffe, Noel Connors and Barry Coughlan. The ancient régime prevails

(4) Stick and helmet discarded, Waterford corner back Noel Connors doesn't try to hide his disappointment after the defeat

2.

(1) Dream debut. Galway substitute Shane Maloney, making his senior debut, scores the winning point to complete a maroon tour de force in the hurling game of the year. They pip Tipp by a point in a thriller

(2) The art of defending. Kerry's Marc Ó Sé makes a crucial full-length block against Connor McAliskey of Tyrone, while goalkeeper Brendan Kealy makes himself big just in case

30 GAA Football All-Ireland Senior Championship Semi-Final - Croke Park, Dublin
Dublin 2-12   Mayo 1-15

5 GAA Football All-Ireland Senior Championship Semi-Final Replay - Croke Park, Dublin
Dublin 3-15   Mayo 1-14

(1) We've been here before. Game level, deep in injury time and Stephen Cluxton swings his left boot at the ball from the right side of the field. However, this time his effort sails wide and Mayo live to fight another day following a semi-final epic

(2) Into the light, still in the limelight. The saga surrounding Diarmuid Connolly's involvement in the semi-final replay against Mayo runs until the early hours of the morning of the game. His appeal goes to the GAA's Disputes Resolution Authority who clear him to play despite his red card in the drawn game

1.   2.

" We engaged with the process. It's there for us, it's there for any team to use and that's what we did. We took advice from the administrators of the Dublin county board and they supported us all the way "

Dublin manager Jim Gavin on Diarmuid Connolly's successful appeal against a one-match ban which allowed Connolly to play in the semi-final replay against Mayo

6 Electric Ireland GAA Hurling All-Ireland Minor Championship Final - Croke Park, Dublin
Galway 4-13 Tipperary 1-16

1.

(1) Maor Square. GAA president Aogán Ó Fearghail and director general Páraic Duffy pose with volunteer stewards on the day of the All-Ireland hurling final. A selection of the same group form an integral part of the Croke Park match-day team for every fixture at the venue

(2) Triumphant Tribesman. Galway minor hurling captain Seán Loftus raises the Irish Press Cup and throws down the gauntlet to the county's seniors

(3) Brought to his knees. Tipperary's Tommy Nolan digests the defeat

6 GAA Hurling All-Ireland Senior Championship Final - Croke Park, Dublin
Kilkenny 1-22   Galway 1-18

1.

(1) A moment in time. Kilkenny and Galway hurlers walk in the pre-match parade and Irish people the world over connect with home. Tension palpable, this is the All-Ireland hurling final. A day like no other

(2) The view from the upper deck. Kilkenny defender Shane Prendergast takes a lift off Galway's Conor Whelan in the battle for supremacy

(3) One-handed pulling. Galway defender Pádraig Mannion shapes to drop his hurley with his right hand as he and Ger Aylward battle for position and possession

6   GAA Hurling All-Ireland Senior Championship Final - Croke Park, Dublin
Kilkenny 1-22   Galway 1-18

2.

3.

4.

(1)   Cheek to cheek. Ger Aylward, off his feet, collides with Galway's Daithí Burke, on his knees. Aylward is one of the Kilkenny finds of the season

(2)   'This one is getting away from us'. Galway manager Anthony Cunningham reacts to a passage of play from the Hogan Stand touchline. The contrast between his team's first and second-half displays could hardly be greater

(3)   The winning habit. Brian Cody strikes a familiar pose on the final whistle as he celebrates his 11th All-Ireland success in 16 years as Kilkenny manager

(4)   The Cat is in the bag. Pádraig Walsh, left, and Lester Ryan celebrate Kilkenny's latest success

6 GAA Hurling All-Ireland Senior Championship Final - Croke Park, Dublin
Kilkenny 1-22 Galway 1-18

1.

2.

(1) Food for thought. There are few things to concentrate the mind like the shrill blow of the referee's final whistle when you're behind on All-Ireland final day. Galway's Jason Flynn tries to make sense of it all

(2) They can't take this away from me. Kilkenny captain Joey Holden joins the illustrious – and growing – club of winning captains from the county

(3) Kilkenny backs to the wall – a novel experience. Rackard Cody, the Kilkenny kit man, places streamers on the victorious players. Even in the dressingroom, there is an aura about the black and amber

" Every year you win the All-Ireland final it's a brilliant feeling and I don't rank them, to be honest. It's just about winning today's match and winning the All-Ireland final is everything **"**

Brian Cody takes it one year at a time as he celebrates a remarkable 11th All-Ireland senior success as Kilkenny manager

3.

12 Bord Gáis Energy GAA Hurling All-Ireland Under-21 B Championship Final - Semple Stadium, Thurles
Wicklow 2-17 Meath 2-15

Bord Gáis Energy GAA Hurling All-Ireland Under-21 Championship Final - Semple Stadium, Thurles
Limerick 0-26 Wexford 1-07

2.

(1 - 2) The winners' enclosure. Wicklow and Limerick celebrate All-Ireland under-21 hurling successes in Thurles. An outstanding Limerick side defeated Wexford and Wicklow pipped Meath in the B championship

SEPTEMBER '15

13 Liberty Insurance All-Ireland Senior Camogie Championship Final - Croke Park, Dublin
Cork 1-13   Galway 0-09

20 Electric Ireland GAA Football All-Ireland Minor Championship Final - Croke Park, Dublin
Kerry 4-14   Tipperary 0-06

1.

2.

(1) Red is the colour. The Cork camogie team line up by the red carpet as they wait for the President, Michael D Higgins. Galway await thereafter

(2) Reach for the sky. Ashling Thompson, the Cork captain, looks to the heavens as she lifts the O'Duffy Cup following her team's impressive win over Galway and her own notable contribution

(3) Rising highest. Tipperary's Tadhg Fitzgerald, left, gets his hands on the ball as he and team-mate Jack Skehan leap above Bryan Sweeney of Kerry in the All-Ireland minor football final. Kerry were flying highest at the finish

(4) One for the future? Kerry captain Mark O'Connor, a class act at midfield, lifts the Tom Markham Cup after their big win over Tipperary

❝ That's the dream come true and it puts the icing on my career. It's everything I have worked for. For everything I've been through in my own life ❞

Cork captain Ashling Thompson after the team's victory over Galway in the All-Ireland senior camogie final

4.

1.

2.

(1) The President, Michael D Higgins, is captured between Kerry forwards Johnny Buckley, left, and Stephen O'Brien in the pre-match formalities

(2) Subbuteo table. The miniature figures of the Dublin and Kerry players may be unrecognisable from this angle but there's no doubt that this is the 2015 All-Ireland football final, thanks in part to the returned final-day pitch artwork

" It was always going to come down to the fine margins. Conditions made it difficult for both sides to play, a lot of errors in it, but we're just very happy we got over the line "

Jim Gavin after Dublin's All-Ireland final win over Kerry

1.

2.

3.

(1) Game changer par excellence. Dublin's rampaging corner back Philly McMahon forces one of the greatest forwards of all time to chase back and defend. Colm Cooper attempts the block but McMahon's shot sails over the bar – and sends out a statement of intent

(2) Gravity defying. The timeless picture of two of the greats, Seán Walsh and Brian Mullins, at full stretch in a 1970s aerial duel now has a rival as Dublin's Brian Fenton and David Moran of Kerry challenge physics in pursuit of possession.

(3) Pay close attention. Substitute Kevin McManamon had burnt Kerry twice in recent big matches, thus ensuring a special plan would await his introduction. That plan – an Aidan O'Mahony man-marking job – was working well until a trip earned the Kerryman a black card

1.

(1) Eyes on the prize. Dublin full back Rory O'Carroll somehow keeps his focus while Stephen Cluxton and Kerry's Paul Geaney momentarily lose sight of the ball in a frantic aerial contest

(2) Gazelle-like. Dublin's James McCarthy, the epitome of the modern-day footballer, holds off Kerry veteran Paul Galvin as Dublin close out the game

2.

20 GAA Football All-Ireland Senior Championship Final - Croke Park, Dublin
Dublin 0-12   Kerry 0-09

(1) The reaction 1. Kerry's Peter Crowley can only watch as Dublin trio Diarmuid Connolly, Ciarán Kilkenny and John Small greet the final whistle.

(2) The reaction 2. Calm and collected v ecstatic and jubilant. Dublin manager Jim Gavin keeps his emotions in check at the final whistle while his selector and former team-mate Mick Deegan lets rip

(3) The reaction 3. The significance of winning a Celtic Cross can be difficult to articulate, as an emotional Kevin McManamon realises despite landing his third

(4) The reaction 4. The deluge continues but it's an irrelevance for the boys in blue. Paul Flynn, left, and Bernard Brogan soak it all up

(5) The reaction 5. After securing the O'Byrne Cup, National League and Leinster championship trophies, Dublin captain Stephen Cluxton gets his hands on the one he wanted most – the Sam Maguire Cup

(6) The reaction 6. Johnny Cash meets Bubba Watson? A Dublin fan sports a cowboy hat and argyle trousers but the colour is true blue. The party is declared on

5.

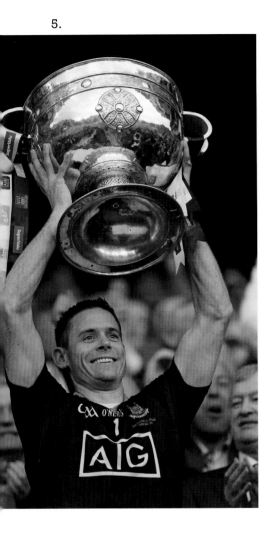

6.

❝ They are different eras. Nothing will ever match Kevin Heffernan's team and what he did for the GAA in Dublin. His spark and genius, we just stand on their shoulders really **❞**

Jim Gavin's reply when asked to compare his lads to Heffo's team of the 1970s

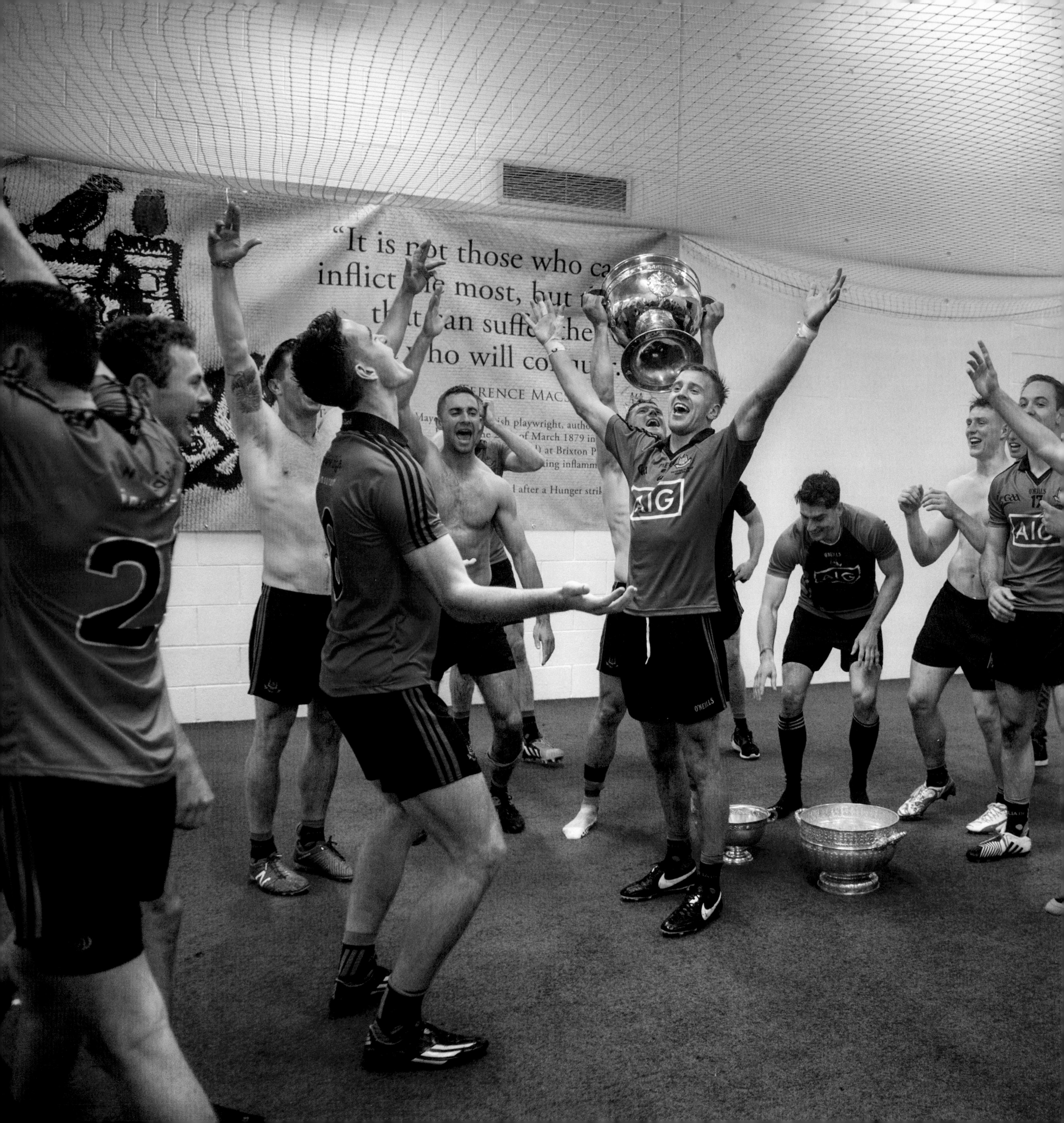
AIG

1.

2.

(1) The shackles are off. Wonderful, chaotic scenes in the Dublin dressingroom as the players let their hair down after a year of outstanding achievement – and sacrifice

(2) The end of the road? A despondent Paul Galvin, who came out of retirement at the age of 35 to give it another shot, is deep in thought – perhaps considering his future in the green and gold

2.

3.

4.

(1) Trigger pulled. Valerie Mulcahy of Cork is all balance and poise as she prepares to shoot in the ladies football senior final. Dublin's Sorcha Furlong closes in

(2) Crowded house. The stakes rise as the clock ticks down and there are leads to protect – or challenge. Few teams are as experienced at closing out a game as the Cork women

(3) The losing lark ain't easy. Dublin's Ciara Trant, right, and Sinéad Goldick console each other after the county's second consecutive final defeat to Cork

(4) Red-letter day. Captain Ciara O'Sullivan, surrounded by team-mates and supporters, confirms Cork's supremacy by raising the Brendan Martin Cup

GALLERY OF FANS

AWARD WINNING IMAGES
sportsfile

Relive all the agony and ecstasy of past campaigns

1997	1998	1999	2000	2001
2002	2003	2004	2005	2006
2007	2008	2009	2010	2011
2012	2013	2014